STORE KIND OF FAITH

FAITH

BY

FAITH

STORE KIND OF FAITH

FAITH

BY

FAITH

By Pamela Tolson

authorHOUSE®

AuthorHouse™
1663 Liberty Drive
Bloomington, IN 47403
www.authorhouse.com
Phone: 1-800-839-8640

COVERED DESIGN:
MELVIN G. & PAMELA TOLSON SR.

All Scriptures quotations are taken from the
King James Version.

Published by AuthorHouse   01/19/2012

ISBN: 978-1-4685-0139-1 (sc)
ISBN: 978-1-4685-0138-4 (e)

Library of Congress Control Number: 2011960542

WORDS OF DEDICATION

First, I give all glory and honor to my Lord and Savior Jesus Christ for making this book possible.

Secondly, I thank my husband, Melvin Sr., who has supported me with his patience and also with helping in the birthing of this project.

Also, I thank my children, Sharon, Melvin Jr., and Renee (Louis), along with their families, my grands, family and friends for their love and support.

I thank my Mom (Gwendolyn) who has always encouraged me in everything that I've always tried to accomplish in life.

I'm also thankful for having attended a dynamic seminar which was given by Pamela JP Martin, Authur of Unique Books, "How to write a book without Crying," and the Editor of "Write 4U" Claudia Tynes who along with my daughters, Sharon and Renee who took the time to edit this book.

Pam

Enjoy your blessings!

Contents

Enjoy your blessings!

INTRODUCTION

This book is written to encourage you that God is always there regardless of where you are or what you are doing; whether in a store or otherwise. God is no respect of person when it comes to having faith in His word; He honors faith. Remember that God loves you just like a father loves his children. Also, remember that when you ask God in the name of Jesus expect by faith that He will answer your prayer. Keep your faith in the Almighty God and see Him as your source. Keep faith in the present (the now).

It gives me joy when I can pray to my heavenly Father, knowing that He loves me and when I pray with my request in Jesus Name, He does it. What a mighty God we serve!

I'm excited to share with you some of my personal testimonies. Perhaps you can relate to some of them.

Enjoy your blessings!

Enjoy your blessings!

STORE KIND OF FAITH

Part I

Enjoy your blessings!

STORE KIND OF FAITH

You will read the results of my many blessings where GOD (and nobody but GOD) has blessed me while purchasing merchandise in the stores. Before purchasing my items, I pray and thank God in the Name of Jesus for my discounts. I'm at the point now that I am looking and expecting God to give me discounts on my purchases.

Come take a journey with me on seven (7) ways in which GOD has blessed me. It gives me great pleasure to share them with you. If He discounts my purchases, surely He loves you as much as He loves me and will do the same thing for you. God honors FAITH.

1. <u>Purchase with Coupon:</u>

There were many times when I did not have a store coupon, and I prayed, "GOD, bless me with one or more coupons to purchase my items." At times the salesperson let me use their coupon and on other occasions, I received a coupon from nice customers who are purchasing their merchandise at the same time.

2 Peter 1:7, "And to godliness brotherly kindness; and to brotherly kindness charity."

Who have you shown kindness to and how did it make that person feel?

_____

_____

_____

_____

2. <u>Purchase in Grocery Store:</u>

While in the grocery store I prayed, "God, give me an impossible discount." When I got to the checkout counter, the cashier stated, "The two boxes of fish cost $1 each." With a look of surprise on my face, she asked the cashier beside her if what I had purchased was $1. He agreed and I paid $1 for each box. It had just dawn on me that I had asked the Lord for an impossible discount. The original cost for both boxes of fish should have been at least $8. I praised God at the counter.

St. John 16: 23, "Whatsoever ye shall ask the Father in my name, he will give it you."

What have you asked the Lord in His name that you thought was impossible?

_____

_____

_____

_____

_____

3. <u>Purchased Truck:</u>

My husband and I were approved for a $20,000 loan to purchase a new vehicle for me. We looked for weeks for the perfect purchase that was within the loan amount, but was unsuccessful. Although I loved the vehicle I was driving so dearly, it was on its last leg. I told the Lord that He knew what vehicle I wanted, and that I knew that He had a truck for me. I gave God the color and what I desired in the truck I wanted to purchase. Well, wouldn't you know as I was driving pass a car dealer, I saw some trucks. It seemed like my husband and I overlooked this particular car dealer. I drove on the lot of the dealership and a truck caught my eye. I test drove it and returned to the car dealer's office to complete the paperwork. Immediately, I saw another vehicle through the window which was a gray truck. It was the exact color that I prayed about. I asked the salesperson,

Purchased Truck: (continued)

"Is the truck available for sale?" He answered, "Yes." Hurriedly, I got in the truck, turned on the radio and Christian music was already playing. I knew within my spirit that this was the vehicle for me. The purchase price for the truck should have been $30K or more. I purchased the truck for $20K plus taxes and tags. The salesman said, "I do not know why I let you have that truck for that price." I smiled at him and praised my God within my spirit.

Matt. 19:26, "With men this is impossible; but with God all things are possible."

What have you purchased that you know it was only possible by God?

_____

_____

_____

_____

4. <u>Purchased my Mom's Blouse:</u>

My mother and I went to a well known department store to purchase a blue-flowered blouse, but the one she wanted was not available in her size. The nice salesperson found the same blouse at another store. Without my mother knowing, one Sunday after church I drove to the other store where the blouse was located. I prayed, "God, in the name of Jesus, show me where the blouse is located in the store." I went to the women's clothing section of the store where blouses were sold. The salesperson, who has worked in this section for a few years, told me that she did not know why they told me they had this blouse because the store did not carry that name brand. She also assured me that she knew her clothing section very well and insisted that this blouse was not in the store. I prayed, "Lord, that blouse is here in this store. Now Lord, you know where it is, but I do not. I thank you in the name of Jesus for telling me where it is ." While talking

Purchased Mom's Blouse: (continued)

to the salesperson at the register, I glanced to her left. As God is my witness, I saw the blouse hanging in front of a clothing rack behind her. I thought, *Oh my God, there's the blouse.* The salesperson was amazed too. Isn't God awesome? Not only did the Lord show me the blouse, He added a special bonus. I was not aware of the coupons for that day until the salesperson offered her coupons to me. She reached into her purse and gave them to me, and I purchased all my merchandise. I surprised my mom with the blouse at her 80th birthday celebration. What a mighty God we serve!

Philippians 4:6, "Be careful for nothing; but in everything by prayer and supplication with thanksgiving let your request be made known unto God."

What have you prayed for lately and the Lord answered your prayer?

_____

_____

_____

_____

5. <u>Purchased Pantsuit</u>:

I went to the store and saw a beautiful brown pantsuit. It was on the same day that I purchased my mom's blouse. The two-piece brown pantsuit had one price for the jacket and another price for the pants. I purchased the pants the same day I purchased my mom's blouse, but I did not buy the jacket. I told the Lord that it was too expensive. I left the jacket in the store with plans on returning at a later date to buy it when it was on sale. Weeks later, one Sunday after service the Lord placed the suit jacket in my spirit. While driving home, I made a "U" turn and went to the department store. The suit jacket was still there with a marked down price of $39 from the original price of $199. I purchased the suit jacket along with other sale merchandise, but with no additional discounts. Don't you think for a minute that I did not ask the Lord about my additional discount. All the items

Purchased Pantsuit: (continued)

purchased the previous week had additional mark downs. After showing the salesperson my receipt, I received discounts on all previous purchases including my suit jacket. Hallelujah!

James 1:6, "But let him ask in faith, nothing wavering. For he that wavereth is like a wave of the sea driven with the wind and tossed."

After you asked the Lord for something, did you have trouble waiting for His answer?

_____

_____

_____

_____

6. <u>Purchased Banquet Suit:</u>

With only $45 in my wallet, I needed an outfit for a banquet that I was attending. So, I prayed, "Lord, you know my taste in clothings." "Thank you for providing my suit in Jesus' name." The second store I entered had a suit on the sales rack that caught my eye. The gold and cream colored suit was beautiful. It was just my style and price which was within $45. God is goooooooood.

2 Corinthians 5:7, "For we walk by faith, not by sight."

Give an example of how you had to walk by faith and not by sight.

_____

_____

_____

_____

7. <u>Purchased Home:</u>

My husband and I purchased our home before we were saved. We believed the Lord for our new home by writing what we wanted in the house on a sheet of paper. Our list included an all brick house with three bedrooms, a bathroom in the master bedroom, hardwood floors, and a basement with a fireplace. The real estate agent showed us several houses. Finally, we found the home that matched our list. We settled for a carport instead of a garage. We believed God even when we did not know to call it **Faith**.

Matthew 21:22, "And all things, whatsoever ye shall ask in prayer, believing, ye shall receive."

What was it that you asked the Lord for and received it?

_____

_____

_____

_____

Enjoy your blessings!

FAITH BY FAITH

Part II

Enjoy your blessings!

FAITH BY FAITH

Because of God's grace and mercy, I can share His love and kindness that He has shown to me through His Word. As you read my testimonies, remember that there is no respect of person with God of those who walk by FAITH. As Christians, in order to live victorious in this life, we must live by FAITH. I am still growing in Christ, and will remain teachable until this life is over. I am a student who loves learning God's Word which forever amazes me. Each time I take a class concerning the Word of God, I realize there is always something I did not know. Come and take another journey with me on my faith walk.

1. <u>Tithes by Faith:</u>

When I first accepted the Lord as my Personal Savior, I did not believe that I could pay 10% of my salary to myself let alone to the church when they taught on tithing. In my eyes, it just was not possible. So I spoke with my Pastor and shared my honest view point about believing that the Bible was right but I did not have 10% to give. I waited for him to tell me what the Bible said about being "cursed with a curse" (Malachi 3:9) if you did not pay your tithes but instead with the wisdom God placed within the Man of God, he said to me, "Daughter, when you get FAITH then you will give your tithes." How many of you know that it takes faith to give 10% of your salary for tithes? My Pastor's answer gave me peace. His response surprised and sparked me to talk to the Lord about tithing. I asked the Lord, "Did you hear what Bishop said, (as if God didn't hear him) when I get faith, then I will give my tithes?" Then I told the Lord with all seriousness that I knew it was right to give 10% of my salary for tithes. So I told the Lord that if he would make a way for me to give 10% of my salary, I would do it. God answered my prayer by giving me a promotion on my job. Then He relocated me to another

Tithes by Faith: (continued)

location with a new position much closer to my home. I have been giving tithes every since that day. It has been over 30 years. It does take faith to give 10% of your salary especially when you first get saved. Financially, you think you really don't have it. God knew my heart, and I believe when I made the right choice to tithe, He made a way.

Exodus 35:5, "Take ye from among you an offering unto the Lord: whosoever is of a willing heart, let him bring it, an offering of the Lord: gold, and silver, and brass, . . ."

When you first heard the teaching on tithing, what was your reaction? Are you giving back 10% of what already belongs to God?

_____

_____

_____

_____

2. <u>Healing by Faith</u>:

One Saturday morning, I decided to drive to the mall. While driving down my street, I saw the cars as doubles. At that time, I was not aware of this being the beginning of an uphill battle. Immediately, I made a "U" turn and drove back to my house. My oldest daughter, who was living with me, was on her way to Chuck E Cheese's with her daughters. She felt something was wrong and returned home to check on me within 15 minutes after me returning home. My daughter took me to the mall while she and the girls went to Chuck E Cheese. While walking in the mall, I realized my vision was double. Everybody and everything I saw was doubled. This really frightened me, and I could not wait to get back home. I had already seen the doctor about the pain I had in my head, but this was in addition to my problem. I called the doctor to speak to him personally, but his assistant returned my call. I was angry because I felt my doctor should have spoken to me. He knew my case and this was a serious matter concerning me. After I hung up the phone, the Lord spoke to me and said, "Put your Trust in me." I told the Lord that I would put my

Healing by Faith: (continued)

trust in Him 100% plus, and I did. It was a spiritual fight, but I told the Lord and others that I will win and not be defeated. This sickness did not come from God, it came from the devil; therefore, I will not accept it. I gave it back to him. While going through my healing process, people told me perhaps you have this or that. I told them I did not have anything. If they wanted those diseases, they could have them, but I did not. Someone also told me to face reality, and I replied that the reality was that I know Jesus. I saw my healing, spoke my healing, and heard my healing. Faith comes by hearing the Word of God. I listened to healing tapes and looked at Christian TV networks. When I read with one eye closed, my vision was single. Finally, I received my final report from the doctor who did not understand what was happening with me. He said that we have taken several vials of blood from you, and some of your tests were extremely good. They gave me two magnetic resonance imagings (MRI), and a spinal tap, but there was no scientific reason for my problem.

Healing by Faith: (continued)

He concluded that whatever it was, it would heal itself. I found a bathroom in the hospital; once inside, I danced and praised my God. Every time someone asked me, "How I was doing?" I said, "I am waiting for the manifestation of my healing." God is true to His Word. I was healed. Hallelujah!

Prayer: "Thank you Lord for everyone who prayed for me while I was going through this sickness. To God be the Glory."

1 Peter 2:24, "Who his own self bare our sins in his own body on the tree, that we, being dead to sins, should live unto righteousness: by whose stripes ye were healed."

Have you ever been healed or do you know someone who has been healed by God? Share your experiences.

_____

_____

_____

_____

3. <u>School by Faith</u>:

During my College Accounting class, the teacher gave the class our first test then he left the room. No one knew how to solve one of the problems which was worth over half of our test score. This would be an automatic 'F' on the test if this problem was not solved. Some of my classmates cheated on the test, and one of them asked me if I wanted them to help me. I answered "No." I turned my paper in knowing that my first test score was an 'F'. Discouraged, I left the classroom. I thought, *"I am a child of God; it is impossible for them to get an 'A' on their papers and I get an 'F.'"* I told another student in the class who also did not cheat that God was going to do something. I prayed concerning this matter. When I returned to class a week after taking the exam, the teacher entered into the classroom, he slammed the door and yelled, "ETHICS." I knew that God had done something. The teacher informed the class that 25 students had the same answer wrong which was obvious to him that there were others

School by Faith: (continued)

in the class who did not cheat on the exam. Therefore, he passed the students who did not cheat. I thanked my God. I got a 'B' out of that class.

Psalms 46:10, "Be still, and know that I am God: I will be exalted among the heathen, I will be exalted in the earth."

Have you ever received a grade in school that you wanted to have changed? Please Explain:

_____

_____

_____

_____

4. <u>Coat by Faith:</u>

My mom and I went on a bus trip to New York to visit my youngest daughter for the weekend. I realized after leaving the terminal from Washington, D.C. that I left my coat in the terminal. I spoke to an employee who was also a bus driver on the bus with us at the time. I asked him if there was a telephone on the bus where he could call the lost and found. He told me that my coat was gone and that I might as well forget it. I told him, "Not my coat, I will get my coat back." He responded, "Do you believe that?" Without any hesitation, "Yes." I went back to my seat after hearing those discouraging words from him and told my mom, "I'm going to get my coat back." Then I asked my mother to excuse me for a moment. I prayed in tongues silently. When I finished, I told my mother, "God is going to give me my coat back." When we arrived in the New York bus terminal, I went into the station and asked if they would call to Washington, D.C. about my coat. There was no coat in the Washington, D.C. Terminal.

Coat by Faith: (continued)

During my stay in New York, I continued praising God for returning my coat to me. I stood on my faith believing God that if I ask anything in His name (Jesus) that He will do it. When I got back to Washington, D.C., I went to the bus terminal's lost and found. I asked if my coat was there. The attendant asked me to describe it. She left the room and when she returned, she gave me my coat. She told me that one of her co-workers had planned to take my coat. I told her to tell whoever tried to take my coat, they could not. My spirit was in that coat. My mother was amazed. She told me after I received my coat that she did not believe that I would get it back. She never shared her views with me until after I received my coat. My mother is so sweet, and she would never discouraged me. You see, I asked God to return something that belonged to me.

Coat by Faith: (continued)

You have that same right to get back what belongs to you. All glory goes to God.

Psalms 46:1, "God is our refuge and strength, a very present help in trouble."

Explain a situation where the Lord was a very present help to you in trouble?

_____

_____

_____

_____

5. <u>Parking by Faith:</u>

Praying for a parking space is the norm for me especially when I know that a particular location has limited parking. One Saturday morning I drove to Virginia to attend a Prayer Breakfast. I was informed that the parking was limited. So I prayed and asked the Lord about free parking. When I arrived at the event, I stopped and asked a young lady about the parking in the area. The young lady directed me to a free parking garage.

Psalms 6:9, "The Lord hath heard my supplication; the Lord will receive my prayer."

When was the last time you prayed and asked the Lord to give you a parking space?

_____

_____

_____

_____

6. <u>Healing by Faith:</u>

Early one Saturday morning, my youngest daughter and I were driving to church. As we were driving on our merry way, a car dashed out in front of my car. I never saw the car coming, but my daughter did; she screamed. After I hit the car, my car drifted to the side of the road. My knee hit the steering column and started swelling. The police and ambulance arrived and asked me if I wanted to go to the hospital; I declined. In my mind, all I could think about was God healing me.

My daughter was shaken up, but she and the driver from the other vehicle were fine. The damage to my car was extensive; it could not be driven home. Thank God, a member from my church stopped to assist me. She took me and my daughter home. When I arrived home, my husband wanted to know why I did not go to the hospital? I told him the Lord was going to heal me. I prayed silently, "Lord, my family do not believe that you will heal me right now; show them Lord." While we all gathered in a circle, we prayed and the Lord healed me instantly. We praised God

Healing by Faith: (continued)

for my healing. After everyone left the room, immediately the pain in my knee worsened. I knew it was the devil trying to make me doubt God concerning my healing. So I called my sister in Christ back into the room. I told her what had happened and said, "Let's rebuke this pain in the Name of Jesus." God healed me, and I will not let the devil take my healing back. We prayed and immediately the pain left my body. Until this day, I have never had that pain. Hold on to your healing because it belongs to you.

Is. 53:4-5, " . . . with his stripes we are healed."

Give your testimony of an instance where the Lord healed your body or someone you know?

_____

_____

7. *Healing by Faith:

I felt the healing power of God moving through my body. My body was in so much pain (flu like symptoms) until I could barely move or walk. I was unable to go to work. One of the sisters from my church drove me to our church's noon day prayer service. My Pastor and other members prayed for me. But when I returned to my home, the pain in my body worsened; however, the pain did not shake my faith. I stood on the Word of God that said, "BY JESUS STRIPES I WAS HEALED." I talked to the Lord about my healing and reminded Him of the His Word. I believed what it said and I was not going to doubt His Word. Immediately, the presence of the Holy Spirit moved from the top of my head down through my body and came out of my feet. I was totally, healed. I praised my God for my healing. I did not care who heard me as I shouted praises to my God.

Is. 53:5, ". . . with his stripes we are healed"

Have you or have you heard of someone else who has experienced this kind of healing?

_____

_____

*This healing was quite different from the other healings in my body. I encourage you to trust God and claim your healing in your body now. Do not allow the enemy to steal your healing. Hold onto the Word of God because with JESUS STRIPES YOU ARE HEALED. Continue praising and thanking God for your healing everyday until the manifestation comes. Trust God and not your symptoms. "The just shall live by his FAITH." (Habakkuk 2:4). God has shown me His power, His love and I am forever grateful. God loves you too.

Other related Scriptures: Psalm 27:13, James 2:26, Hebrews 11:6, Matthew 17:20, Hebrews 10:38, and Proverbs 30:5.

I cannot imagine living my Life without God. Nor could I imagine not being able to call on the Name of Jesus in everything. Enjoy your blessings because you are already blessed in the Name of Jesus.

If you want to be saved today, receive Jesus in your heart. (Romans 10:9-10,13)

<u>Song Lyrics</u>: Only believe, Only believe, all things are possible if you only believe. Jesus He Knows . . .

NOTES: YOUR STORE KIND OF FAITH

Part I

_____

_____

_____

_____

_____

_____

_____

_____

_____

_____

_____

_____

_____

_____

NOTES: YOUR STORE KIND OF FAITH

Part I

_____

_____

_____

_____

_____

_____

_____

_____

_____

_____

_____

_____

_____

_____

_____

_____

NOTES: YOUR STORE KIND OF FAITH

Part I

NOTES: YOUR STORE KIND OF FAITH

Part I

NOTES: YOUR FAITH BY FAITH

Part II

_____

_____

_____

_____

_____

_____

_____

_____

_____

_____

_____

_____

_____

_____

_____

NOTES: YOUR FAITH BY FAITH

Part II

NOTES: YOUR FAITH BY FAITH

Part II

NOTES: YOUR FAITH BY FAITH

Part II

Enjoy your blessings!